Spiritual Journey:
Finding My Way

JAE'LY
Poetry

Spiritual Journey:Finding My Way Volume 1© 2022 by Jasmine Morgan. All rights reserved. Printed in the United States of America. No part of this book may be used or reproduced in any manner without written permission by JAE'LY Poetry.

www.jaelypoetry.net

Published by JAE'LY Poetry

ISBN:9798358003941

Illustration: Jasmine Morgan
Author: Jasmine Morgan

Acknowledgements

I would like to thank God for everything he has done in my life. I know without him this book would have not been possible. I would like to thank my mom for always believing, pushing, and encouraging me to write. Candy Publishing for giving me the resources to help publish this book. Chris Manion for encouraging me to do the 21 days 21 poems challenge, and Word Weavers poetry group for their critiques. I would like to dedicate this book to my best friend, Fredrica Spivey who is no longer with us. She was always pushing and encouraging me to write. Thank you to everyone that has helped me make this possible, even the people reading this book.

Have you ever questioned your existence or started on a journey but were lost along the way? Journeys are never easy when we are faced with obstacles. All of us have been in a place where we did not recognize ourselves. This book may speak about my journey, but it is also for people that may have felt the same way or have similar stories. Often, we think no one understands us or no one has had similar stories. This book is for everyone. No matter the circumstance you face, you will see that we are all trying to find those missing pieces we lost along the journey. When reading this book, you will see there is light at the end of my journey. I pray you will have found your light by the time you finish this book. I hope this journey will enlighten, bless, encourage, and inspire someone to keep going on their journey.

Spiritual Journey: Finding My Way

Volume 1

Poems and Illustrations
by Jasmine Morgan

Table of Contents

- Questions 2
  - Pieces 4
  - Puzzling the Pieces 5
  - My Way 6
  - Running 7
    - Wrong Dive 9
    - Crash 10
    - Pain 11
    - Defeat 12
      - Weather 14
      - Sunny Day 15
      - Loving Embrace 16
    - Small Voice 18
    - His Hands 19
    - Here? 20
  - Another Dive 22
  - Submerged 23-24
  - Emerge 25
  - Joy 26
- Answers 28
- Reflection 29

Sometimes we lose our way only to find missing pieces of ourselves...

Questions

Unbelief, doubt,
questioning my existence on this Earth.

Am I alive?
Is this a mere dream of mine?

If I die, will I reincarnate?
Do I disperse
into an empty dark universe?

Questions about spiritual capabilities.
Maybe there's a God or a big bang theory.

How do I exist in this world?

Assume it's for a purpose
But who created the universe?

I still question my existence on Earth.

Pieces

Lost...
Searching for missing pieces.
trying to remember who I was
before...

Pieces fell with each tragic event
scattered in many places
leaving the remnant of my lighthearted joy.
Pieces still falling!
Am I making this worse?
Broken and hurt
still figuring out my self-worth.
A long overdue quest
in need of spiritual guidance.

Lost...
Searching for missing pieces
trying to remember who I was
before...

Puzzling the Pieces

Feet firmly planted in the ground.
Turning on my chakras to help me on my quest.
Who am I?
Maybe Astrology's the best solution.
Showing me, what I am capable of being.
Will they fill the missing pieces?
Let's just cut to the chase.
Astrology's a bunch of nonsense.
Perhaps if I watch a reader predict the future
They can help me find my missing pieces.
Who am I?
Jumping from different spiritual guidance.
Broken!
Who can puzzle the pieces?

My Way

I know who I need,
But my stubbornness will not allow me to submit to the King.
I want to continue doing my own thing.
—Spending hours hanging with crowds
And bad influencers—
I know who I need,
But my stubbornness will not allow me to submit to the King.

Running

Constantly running
Knowing I was called to do something
Not knowing
About that something
I keep running
Scared
The plans I made are not the plans He has for me
I want to do my own thing
Live and be who I want to be

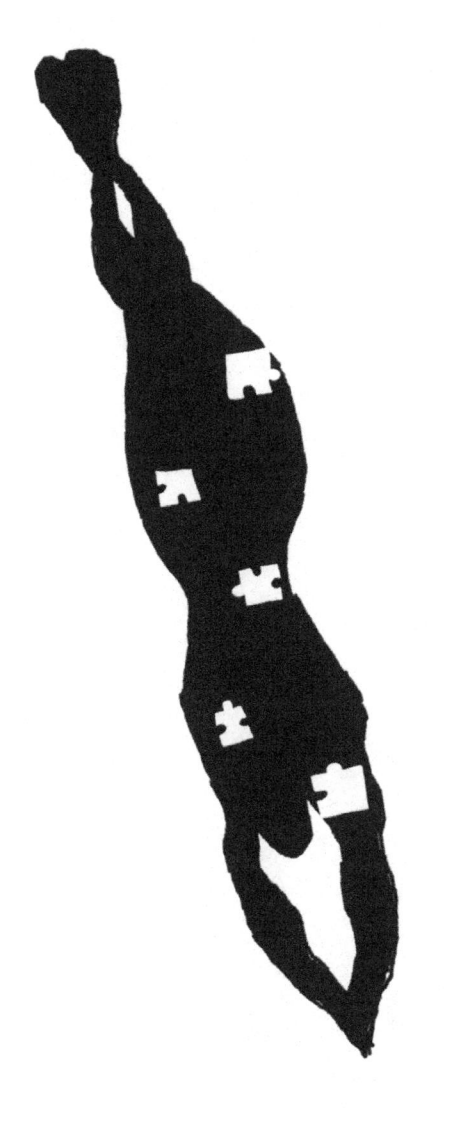

Wrong Dive

Why should I submit to the King?
If I can't live how I want

Dive Deep
Headfirst
Don't think
Just go
Close eyes
Deep breath
Jump
Tuck
Release
Stretch arms
Open eyes
A mistake
Hard fall
Crash!

Crash

Crash!
What was I thinking?
Maybe I wasn't thinking at all.
Listening to my own flesh
Did not help at all.

It hurts.

Dive Deep.
Headfirst.
That was not the best approach.

Worst of all
I landed in an empty arena
no water to help my fall.

What was I thinking?
Maybe I wasn't thinking at all.

Pain

Agony,
Sharp pain piercing through my veins
Is this the end?

Defeat

Heartache
Pain
Stress
Depression
Trying to figure it out on my own
Confusion
Left in the dark alone
Cornered by everything
A wall formed
Trapped in my own mess
No way out
Not even a door
To lead me to
Another exit
Defeated
I sit with my head hanging low

Weather

Believing I can accomplish a lot on my own
Becoming weary of the façade of holding it all together
I cannot stand another stormy weather

Sunny Day

Head down
As tears stream my face
Clouds invading my space
Pleading for help
To take away the pain
I have nothing left
But sorrows of rain
My God
Can you give me a sunny day?

Loving Embrace

No way will I be accepted
in His loving embrace.

A sunny day?
Who am I kidding?
I made a mistake.
I messed up,
I do not deserve His grace.

Instead, He should throw me away
And never look back.

Running away and leaving Him...
I'm pretty sure He is mad.
If He decides to throw me away
I will understand.

No way will I be accepted
in His loving embrace.

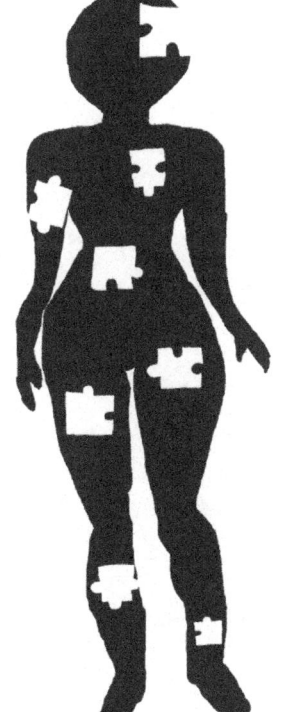

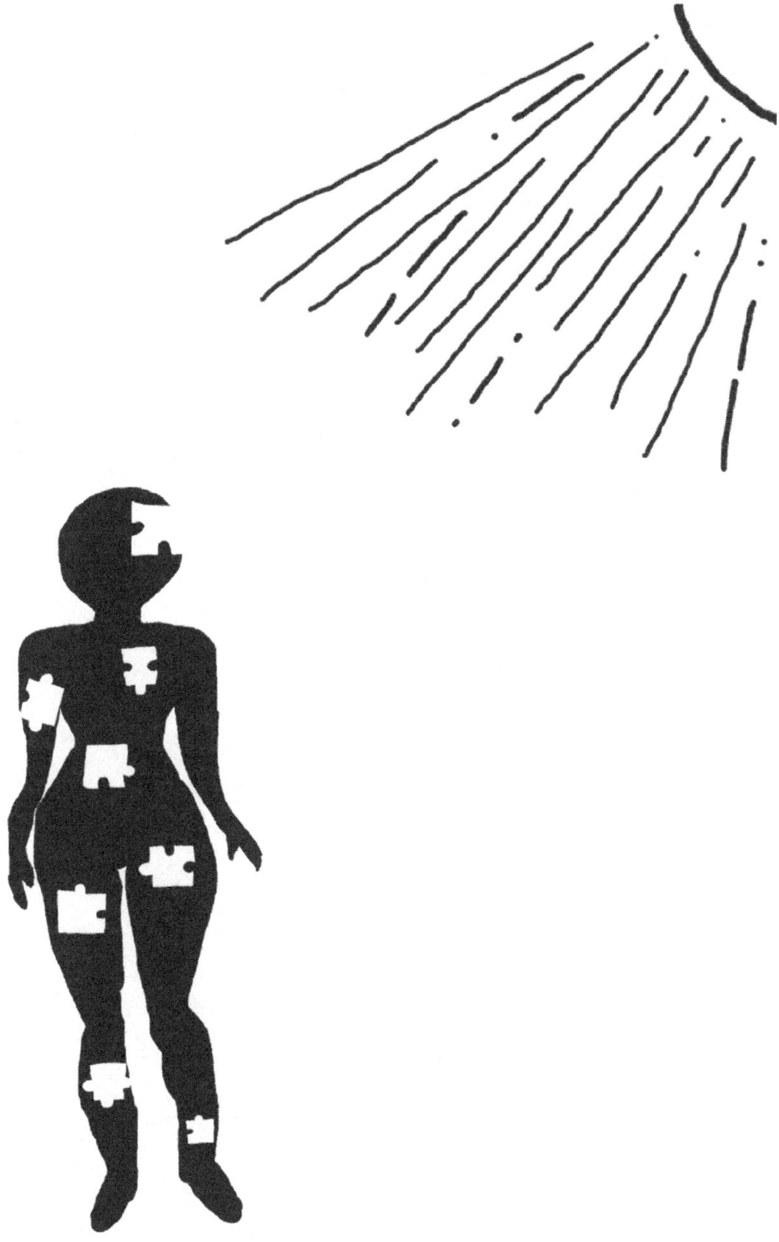

Small voice

My darling
I will always love you
A seed planted
I know all that you will come to be
Each day is already for seen
For the plan I have for you
Is greater beyond any means
As you can see
I still love you
Even though you left me

His Hands

All this time I tried to take matters
Into my own hands
Knowing God has a plan
To help me understand
My life is in His hands

My life may have been
Scattered into pieces
I lost my identity
Fell face forward
But my life is in His hands

Here?

Where do I go from here?

I don't know how to love You
Teach me to love You
To want nothing else
But be surrounded by You

Where do I go from here?

A reflection
Between
The water and I
Am I making the right choice?

Where do I go from here?

I guess I will have to
Jump
And see

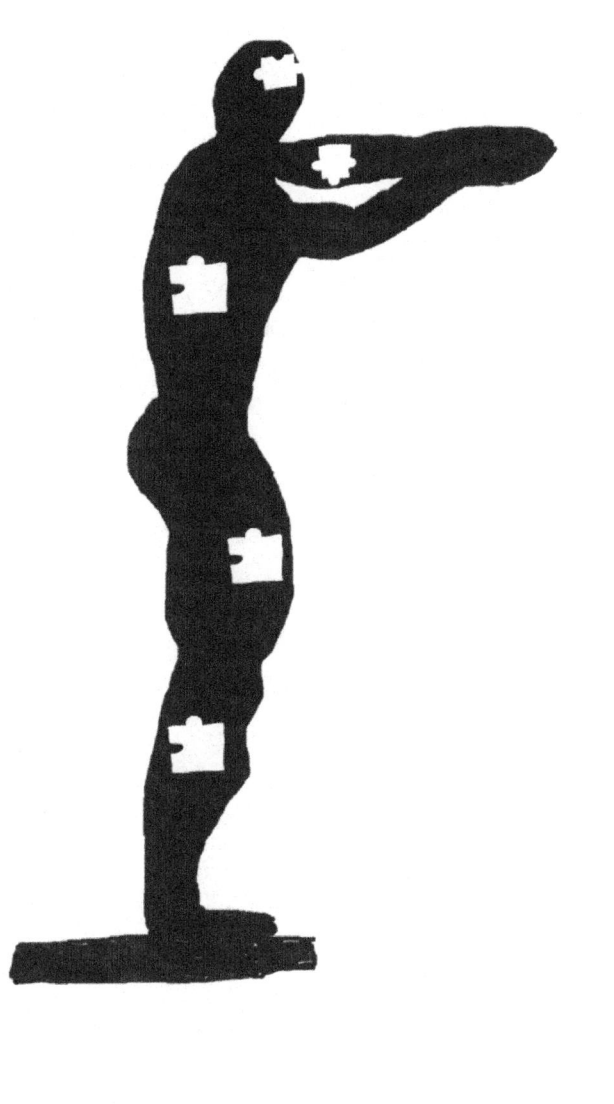

Another Dive

Nothing seemed to work before
Should I trust Him?

Dive deep
Headfirst
Close Eyes
Deep breath
Jump
Release
Arms stretched
Open eyes
Can't wait
Deep breath
Submerge
Into
His loving
Embrace

Submerged

Submerged under
Pieces that were long forgotten
Appeared from the bottom
— of the arena—

Like little piranhas
They were fast
Like leeches
they latched on

Each piece connected
In their rightful place
Even new pieces emerged
Connected to old pieces

Helps keep them in place
With each connection
The pieces faded
—in the skin—

Then I knew I made the right
choice
To take a dive
One more time

Emerge

Refresh
Renew
Confident

Seeing the world in a different view
As I emerge from the water
A light shines bright
Skin glowing
Joy sparkled on my face

Confident
Renew
Refresh

I am happier
With You

Joy

Joyous spirit He brings
My heart dances and sings
When I think about how good He has been
He helps find and mend
My missing
Pieces

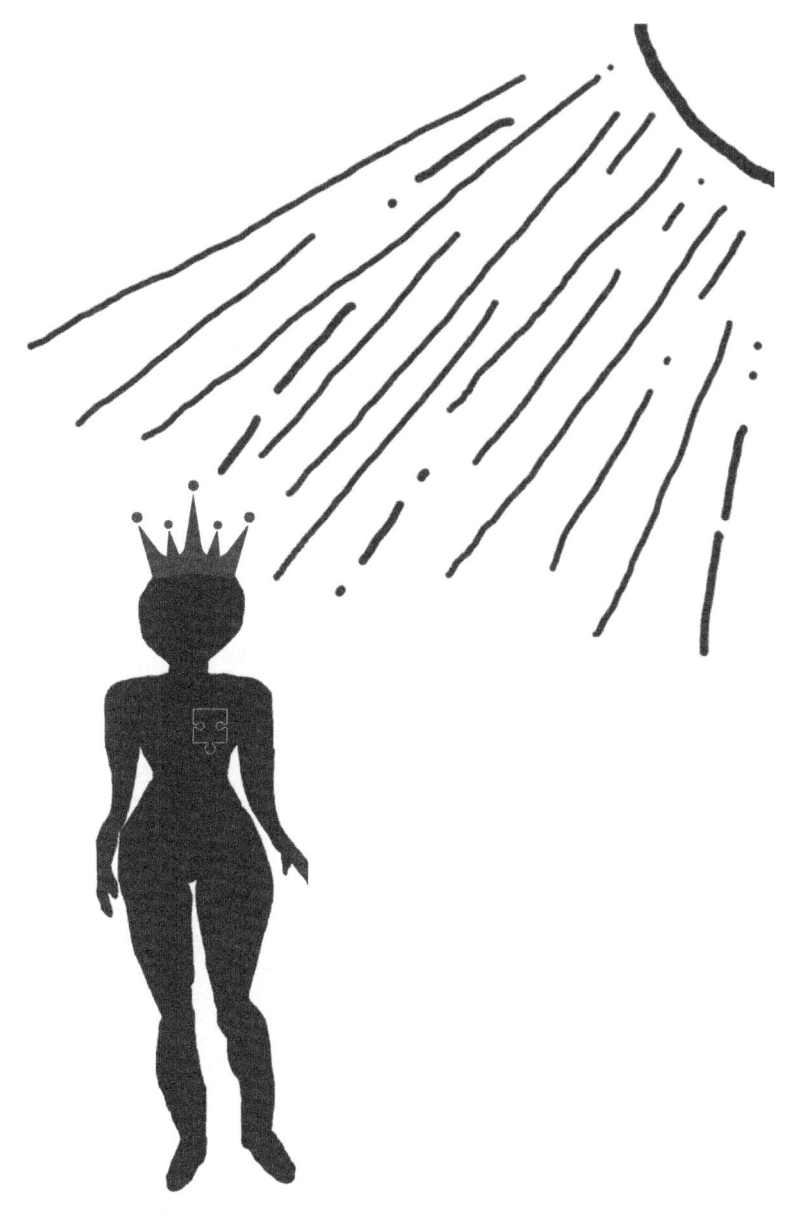

Answers

I know who I am
A child of God

I have a purpose
In this universe

A child of God
I stand
Crown on my head
Held high

No storm can withstand
My existence on this land

I know who I am
A child of God

Alive in Him
No longer questioning my thoughts
I am His child
He is my God

Reflection

I thought I knew it all
Searching for answers
Trying to figure out my own identity
Never wanted to look for the answers
From the one who created my identity
Crashing into concrete
Cornered by my own anguish
Doubting God would ever love me again
Healing took place
Freeing me from my sins
But this is not where my journey ends

Psalm 119:105 "Your word is a lamp for my feet, a light on my path." NIV

Made in the USA
Coppell, TX
15 February 2026

72015677R10039